FRENCH WIT AND WISDOM

Drawings by Fritz Kredel

THE PETER PAUPER PRESS

MOUNT VERNON, NEW YORK

FRENCH WIT AND WISDOM

BEING SAYINGS OF
ROCHEFOUCAULD, BALZAC
CHAMFORT, JOUBERT, VOLTAIRE
SAND, DE STAEL, DE VALOIS
AND STENDHAL

François de la Rochefoucauld	1613-1680
Honoré de Balzac	1799-1850
Sébastien Chamfort	1741-1794
Joseph Joubert	1754-1824
François M. A. de Voltaire	1694-1778
Georges Sand	1804-1876
Madame de Staël	1766-1817
Marguerite de Valois	1553-1615
Stendhal (Henri Beyle)	1783-1842

Rochefoucauld

PASSION often makes fools of clever men; sometimes even makes clever men of fools.

A clever man should organize his self-interests in the order of their worth. Greediness often defeats its own ends, by making us scratch for every trifle when we should dig for gold alone.

Self-interest speaks all tongues and plays all roles; even that of disinterest.

Man's joy or sorrow depends as much upon his disposition as upon his fate.

There is but one Love, yet his shape is legion.

If there be a pure love, free from taint of other passions, it is hidden so deep in our hearts that we are not aware of it ourselves.

Since man does not command his love, no lover should demand constancy of his mistress, nor should she of him.

If we judge love by its results, it is more like hatred than affection.

Enthusiasm is the most convincing orator; it is like the functioning of an infallible law of nature. The simplest man, fired with enthusiasm, is more persuasive than the most eloquent without it.

Clemency, usually considered a royal virtue, comes sometimes from vanity, sometimes from laziness, often from fear; usually from all three combined.

The prosperous are peaceful: good fortune soothes the temper.

6

We all have strength to bear the misfortunes of our neighbors.

Death and the sun are two things no man can outstare.

People are often vain of their most criminal passions; but envy is one passion so mean and low that nobody will admit to it.

Pride is its own support; it loses nothing when vanity is cast away.

Had we ourselves no faults we should find less pleasure discovering them in others.

It is far easier to find a woman who has not sinned at all, than a woman who has sinned but once.

No accident so grave but that the clever man can turn it to some good; no luck so great but that the fool can twist it to his hurt.

Self-interest blinds some men, and makes others see the light.

To establish their position in the world, men go to any length to appear established already.

Jealousy thrives on doubt; certainty drives it to fury, or ends it altogether.

Explore as we may in the vast regions of self-esteem, undiscovered territories remain there still.

We promise according to our hopes, and perform according to our fears.

Conceal our passions as we may under the long cloaks of piety and of honor, still will the cloven hoof peep out.

The generosity of princes is often only policy: to buy the friendship of their people.

Our passions are so surely governed by injustice and self-interest that they are dangerous guides; particularly suspect them when they appear most logical.

Conceit endures less kindly censure of our taste than of our judgment.

Men are prone to forget benefits and injuries; they even learn to hate those who have helped them, and to forget those who have hurt them. The duty of gratitude or revenge is a slavery to which they will not submit.

We praise in others what we find in ourselves; true friendship grows when our self-esteem is flattered by mutual agreement in tastes and pleasures.

8

Sincerity is an open heart. Few people show it; usually what we see is an imitation put on to snare the confidence of others.

True love is like a ghost: everyone talks of it, but few have met it face to face.

In most men the love of justice to all is but the fear of injustice to themselves.

To be deceived by your friends is no disgrace; to distrust them is.

Our self-esteem judges the worth of others by the pleasure their friendship gives us; we measure their merit by their treatment of us.

Every one blames his memory; no one blames his judgment.

Old men love to give good advice; it consoles them for being able no longer to set a bad example.

A great name degrades rather than exalts those unworthy to bear it.

Men and their actions must be seen in proper perspective; some are judged best close at hand, some at a distance.

One form of coquetry is the boast of never flirting.

The blemishes of the mind, like those of the face, increase with age.

We never forgive a betrayal by a friend or by a foe; yet often we are content to betray ourselves.

We work so consistently to disguise ourselves to others that we end by being disguised to ourselves.

If we conquer our passions it is more through their weakness than our strength.

Often we exaggerate the goodness of others more for our own virtue in giving praise than for the virtues which we praise: thus we invite commendation by seeming to dispense it.

Our wish to deserve the praise given us sharpens our merits; praise of our wisdom, our bravery or our beauty tends to increase them.

We would rather speak ill of ourselves than not speak of ourselves at all.

Deprived of the company of fools, a great wit does not seem half so clever.

We often boast that we are never boring to ourselves; our vanity prevents us from seeing how boring we can be to others.

Virtue in women is often the love of a good reputation or a peaceful conscience.

Folly follows us through life; we call that man wise whose folly is in proportion to his age, and to his wealth.

The man who never gives way to folly is not as wise as he thinks.

Perfect valor is to do without witnesses what you would do before the world.

Hypocrisy is the homage vice pays to virtue.

Vanity, shame, and disposition above all, make men brave and women chaste.

Pride more often than ignorance makes us refuse to accept new ideas: finding the first places taken in the intellectual parade, we refuse to take the last.

No one should be praised for goodness who has not strength for wickedness. Most goodness is but laziness or lack of will.

In most men loyalty is a device of self-interest; a means of exalting themselves, and of becoming the depositaries of valuable trusts.

There are some whose faults do them honor; some whose virtues disgrace them.

Gravity is an imposing carriage of the body designed to conceal the absence of the mind.

We always like our admirers; we do not always like those we admire.

What we call liberality is often the vanity of giving — a thing we like more than the thing we give away.

A narrow mind begets obstinacy; it is hard to be persuaded of something beyond the scope of our understanding.

Absence extinguishes small passions and increases great ones, just as a wind will snuff out a candle or fan a fire.

We exaggerate the affection of our friends less in gratitude to them than in exaltation of ourselves.

Some lies are so well disguised to resemble truth, that we should be poor judges of the truth not to believe them.

Nearly everyone is pleased to acknowledge a small indebtedness; many are grateful in acknowledging a moderate one; but there is hardly a man who does not, for a really great indebtedness, return ingratitude.

When men enumerate our virtues they tell us nothing new.

We forgive people who bore us; never those we bore.

Self-interest, blamed for all our ill deeds, should often be praised for our good ones.

We do not open our hearts completely to our friends: not from distrust of them but from distrust of ourselves.

Lovers never tire of each other: they speak always of themselves.

How is it that our memory is good enough to remember the slightest triviality in our lives, but not good enough to remember how often we have told it to the same person.

Jealousy comes more from self-love than from true love.

The extreme delight we take in talking about ourselves should make us suspect that it is not shared by those who listen.

Moderation has been made a virtue so as to curb the ambition of the great, and console the ordinary for their small fortunes and small deserts.

We all know that it is bad taste to talk about our wives; not all of us realize that it is worse to talk about ourselves.

To praise princes for virtues they do not possess is a way to insult them with impunity.

It is particularly hard to break off an affair, when the love that began it is dead.

A gentleman may love like a lunatic, but not like a beast.

There are certain vices which, when well mounted, glitter like the jewel virtue itself.

There are but few virtuous women who are not weary of the part.

Most chaste women are like hidden treasures; safe, because no one is searching for them.

The stresses of fortune, like a lamp, bring out our vices and virtues into bold relief.

If we must fight ourselves to remain faithful to a mistress, we might as well not be.

What we call our sincerity is mostly the desire to talk about ourselves, and to put our faults in the best possible light.

We should manage fortune like our health: enjoy it when it is good, be patient when it is bad, and resort to heroic remedies only in extremity.

Each age of life is new to us; no matter how old we are we still are troubled by inexperience.

Sometimes we think we dislike flattery: we dislike only the method.

Fortune seems most blind to those on whom she has never turned her face.

When other men are caught in our snares we do not think them so foolish: but how ridiculously foolish we seem to ourselves when we are caught in theirs.

If people could see our motives, we should often be ashamed of our noblest actions.

We often think we bear misfortunes with dignity, whereas really we are too stunned to move; we suffer without daring to look our troubles in the eye, like a coward killed because he is afraid to defend himself.

It is easy to forgive in our friends those vices they do not inflict upon us.

We credit ourselves with the vices we do not have: thus if we are weak, we boast of our obstinacy.

Women in love will more readily forgive a great infidelity than a little indiscretion.

In the old age of love, just as in the old age of life, we find we have survived for discomforts, not for joys.

Women are little given to friendship, for it is insipid after love.

We make a virtue of the vices we do not want to correct.

The same pride which makes us condemn the vices from which we think ourselves free, makes us belittle the virtues we know we lack.

Those who have experienced the pain of a great passion bewail their cure the rest of their days.

Age is a tyrant that forbids, under pain of death, enjoyment of the pleasures of youth.

In their first passion women love their lovers; in later passions they love love.

Some people are so self-centered that even in love they manage to be pre-occupied with their own passion to the exclusion of their beloved.

Jealousy is the worst of our ills; but it is the least pitied by those who cause it.

Balzac

It is easier to be a lover than a husband, for the same reason that it is more difficult to be witty every day, than now and then.

What saves the virtue of many a woman is that protecting god, the *Impossible*.

A woman full of faith in the one she loves is but a novelist's fancy.

Money knows nobody; money has no ears; money has no heart.

The man who enters his wife's dressing-room is either a philosopher, or a fool.

Everything is two-faced — even virtue.

The more one judges, the less one loves.

No man has yet discovered the means of successfully giving friendly advice to women — not even to his own.

Marriage should combat without respite or mercy that monster which devours everything — habit.

Between two beings susceptible to love, the duration of love depends upon the first resistance of the woman, or the obstacles that society puts in their way.

Nothing proves better the necessity of an indissoluble marriage than the instability of passion.

Love is a game at which one always cheats.

A lover has all the virtues, and all the defects, that a husband has not.

Marriage often unites for life two people who scarcely know each other.

A man who can love deeply is never utterly contemptible.

When all that is fond in our nature is most thoroughly awakened, when we feel most deeply and tenderly — even then, love is so conscious of its instability that we are irresistibly prompted to ask: Do you love me? Will you love me always?

Passion raises the nervous tension of a woman to the ecstatic pitch at which presentiment is as acute as the insight of a clairvoyant.

Discouragement is of all ages: in youth it is a presentiment, in old age a remembrance.

The man who can govern a woman can govern a nation.

The mistakes of woman result almost always from her faith in goodness, and her confidence in truth.

A weapon is anything that can serve to wound; and sentiments are perhaps the most cruel weapons man can employ to wound his fellow man.

To give birth to a desire, to nourish it, to develop it, to increase it, to irritate it, to satisfy it: this is a whole poem.

Weak souls are capable of only weak sentiments; strong souls of powerful sentiments.

In courting women, many dry wood for a fire that will not burn for them.

Conjugal Love should never put on or take off his eye-bandage but at an opportune time.

In love, a woman is like a lyre that surrenders its secrets only to the hand that knows how to touch its strings.

Every woman carries in the depths of her soul a mysterious weapon, *instinct* — that virgin instinct, incorruptible, which requires her neither to learn, to reason, nor to know, which binds the strong will of man, dominates his sovereign reason, and pales our little scientific candles.

A woman at middle age retains nothing of the pettiness of youth; she is a friend who gives you all the feminine delicacies, who displays all the graces, all the prepossessions which Nature has given to woman to please man; but who no longer sells these qualities.

Marriage has its unknown great men, as war has its Napoleons, poetry its Chéniers, and philosophy its Descartes.

When women love us, they forgive us everything, even our crimes; when they do not love us, they give us credit for nothing, not even for our virtues.

In love, one must not attack a place unless one storms it.

Woman lives by sentiment, man by action.

The world ceases to be a pleasure when it ceases to be a speculation.

It costs more to satisfy a vice than to feed a family.

A woman is a well-served table, that one sees with different eyes before and after the meal.

It is necessary to be almost a genius to make a good husband.

Woman is a creature between man and the angels.

The laws of love unite man and woman so strongly that no human laws can separate them.

Marriage is a treaty in which the conditions should be mutual.

When two beings are united by love, all social conventionalities are suspended.

It is as absurd to pretend that one can not love the same woman always, as to pretend that a good artist needs several violins to execute a piece of music.

Love is the poetry of the senses.

A lover is a herald who proclaims the merit, the wit, or the beauty of a woman: what does a husband proclaim?

Woman is the altar of love.

One is never criminal in obeying the voice of Nature.

Women are demons that make us enter hell through the door of paradise.

Bachelors are the freebooters of marriage.

Woman is a charming creature who changes her heart as easily as her gloves.

Gratitude is an idiotic word; it is put in the dictionary, but it does not exist in the human heart.

Marriage is a science.

Most women proceed like the flea, by leaps and jumps.

Love is the union of a want and a sentiment.

22

Men are like that — they can resist sound argument and yield to a glance.

Women, when they are not in love, have all the cold blood of an experienced attorney.

An inheritance needs as much looking after as a pretty woman, and for lack of care both may slip through the fingers.

When there is an old maid in the house, a watch-dog is unnecessary.

A man's own vanity is a swindler that never lacks a dupe.

A young man loves the first woman who flatters him.

I know something of these sunsets. —They last ten minutes in the sky, and ten years in a woman's heart.

Women know how to say everything among themselves, and more of them are ruined by each other than corrupted by men.

Believe everything you hear said of the world; nothing is too impossibly bad.

Your true man of business regards an author with mixed feelings, in which alarm and curiosity are blended with compassion.

Women, when they have made a sheep of a man, always tell him that he is a lion with a will of iron.

A young man's flirtations do not damage his fortune; but when a man is fifty, the Graces claim payment. At that age love becomes a vice; insensate vanities come into play.

Parents may hinder their children's marriage, but children cannot interfere with the insane acts of their parents in their second childhood.

Women better understand spending a fortune than making one.

The difference between a girl and a married woman is so vast that the girl can no more comprehend it than the married woman can go back to girlhood again.

Love is a vast business, and they who succeed in it should have no other.

Happiness is worth more than all the brilliant things, true and false, that are said every evening in Paris.

The innocence of a girl is like milk which is turned by a thunder-clap, by an evil smell, by a hot day, or even by a sigh.

Chamfort

WE HAVE three kinds of friends: those who love us, those who are indifferent to us, and those who hate us.

Women of the world never use harsh expressions when condemning their rivals. Like the savage, they hurl elegant arrows, ornamented with feathers of purple and azure, but with poisoned points.

The most completely lost of all days is the one on which we have not laughed.

The world either breaks or hardens the heart.

To despise money is to dethrone a king.

Intelligent people make many blunders, because they never believe the world to be as stupid as it is.

The change of fashions is the tax that the industry of the poor levies on the vanity of the rich.

An indiscreet man is an unsealed letter: every one can read it.

Society is composed of two great classes: those who have more dinners than appetite, and those who have more appetite than dinners.

A lover is a man who endeavors to be more amiable than it is possible for him to be: this is the reason why almost all lovers are ridiculous.

There is no sweeter repose than that which is bought with labor.

The loves of some people are but the result of good suppers.

One is more honest in youth, and to the age of thirty years, than when one has passed it. It is only after that age that one's illusions are dispelled. Until then, one resembles the dog that defends the dinner of his master against other dogs: after this period, he takes his share of it with the others.

To live without bitterness, one must turn his eyes toward the ludicrous side of the world, and accustom himself to look at men only as jumping-jacks, and at society as the board on which they jump.

Society would be a charming thing if we were only interested in one another.

Qualities of a too superior order render a man less adapted to society. One does not go to market with big lumps of gold; one goes with silver or small change.

In love, one who ceases to be rich begins to be poor.

There are principles excellent for certain firm and energetic characters, which would be worth nothing for those of an inferior order.

There are more fools than sages; and among the sages, there is more folly than wisdom.

Love is the sweetest and best of moralists.

In experiencing the ills of nature, one despises death; in learning the evils of society, one despises life.

He who allows his happiness to depend too much on reason, who submits his pleasures to examination, and desires enjoyments only of the most refined nature, too often ends by not having any at all.

I esteem the world as much as I can, and still I esteem it but little.

There are more people who wish to be loved than there are who are willing to love.

The worst of all misalliances is that of the heart.

Love pleases more than marriage, for the same reason that a novel is more interesting than a history book.

It is with happiness as with watches: the less complicated, the less easily deranged.

False modesty is the most reputable of all impostures.

One can not imagine how much cleverness is necessary not to be ridiculous.

Enjoy and give enjoyment, without injury to thyself or to others: this is true morality.

To please, one must make up his mind to be taught many things which he already knows, by people who do not know them.

Mothers are the only goddesses in whom the whole world believes.

Celebrity is the chastisement of merit, and the punishment of talent.

Celebrity: the advantage of being known to those who do not know us.

Pleasure may come of illusion, but happiness can come only of reality.

The wealthiest man is he who is most economical; the poorest is he who is most miserly.

The best philosophy to employ toward the world is to alloy the sarcasm of gaiety with the indulgence of contempt.

He who can not govern his passions should kill them, as we kill a horse when we can not master it.

Love is a malicious blind boy, who seeks to blind the eyes of his guide, that both may go astray together.

Man under present social conditions seems to me corrupted more by his reason than by his passions. His passions — I mean those that characterize the primitive man — have preserved for society the few natural elements it still possesses.

Generosity is but the pity of noble souls.

Life is a disease of which sleep relieves us; it is but a palliative: death is the remedy.

Vanity is often the motive that forces a man to summon up all the energy of his soul. Wood added to a steel point makes a dart, two feathers added to wood make an arrow.

The loss of illusions is the death of the soul.

Nearly all men are slaves for the same reason the Spartans assigned for the servitude of the Persians: lack of power to pronounce the syllable, *No*. To be able to utter that word and to live alone, are the only two means to preserve one's freedom and one's character.

When I hear it argued that, taking everything into account, the least sensitive folk are the happiest, I remember the Indian proverb: "Better to be seated than standing, better to be lying than seated, but better than all else to be dead."

At every stage of life he reaches, man finds himself but a novice.

Prejudice, vanity, calculation: these are what govern the world.

I remember to have seen a man forsaking the society of ballet girls because, so he said, he had found them as deceitful as honest women.

What makes the success of many books consists in the affinity there is between the mediocrity of the author's ideas and those of the public.

One must make the choice between loving women and knowing them; there is no middle course.

There is no history worthy of attention save that of free nations; the history of nations under the sway of despotism is no more than a collection of anecdotes.

Some one has said that to plagiarize from the ancients is to play the pirate beyond the Equator, but that to steal from the moderns is to pick pockets at street corners.

'Tis easier to make certain things legal than to make them legitimate.

I ask M. N — why he had ceased to go into society. "Because," he replied, "I no longer love the women and I know the men."

There are well-dressed foolish ideas just as there are well-dressed fools.

Women only give to friendship what they borrow from love.

Love as it exists in society is nothing more than the exchange of two fancies and the contact of two epidermises.

A man in love who pities the reasonable man seems to me like one who reads fairy tales and jeers at those who read history.

Marriage and the celibacy of priesthood both have their drawbacks: be wise in time and make your choice of something which is not irremediable.

Joubert

REMORSE is the punishment of crime, repentance its expiation. The first signifies a troubled conscience, the second a soul changed for the better.

Space is the stature of God.

Piety is a kind of modesty. It makes us turn away our thoughts, as modesty causes us to turn away our eyes, before the forbidden.

We use up in the passions the stuff that was given us for happiness.

It is God's will that we should love even His enemies.

Man pictures God like himself — the indulgent man worships an indulgent God, the stern man a stern God.

Before God man must be neither learned nor philosophical, but a child, a slave, a pupil — at most, a poet.

What is called the *soul* never changes; but what is called the *mind* changes at every age, with every situation, every day. The mind is mobile, varying with the direction of whatever wind blows upon it.

Intellect provides us with many useless thoughts; good sense provides us with necessary ideas.

Some find activity only in repose; others find repose only in movement.

The ancients said "our ancestors" where we say "our descendants." 'Tis the magic of the future and not of the past that attracts us.

The worst phase of error is not falseness, but willfulness, blindness, and passion.

Without duty life is soft and spineless: it cannot hold itself in shape.

Sincere and simple minds can never be more than half mistaken.

Reflection is to color what echo is to sound.

Statesmanship is the art of knowing and leading the multitude, or the majority. Its glory is to lead them, not where they want to go, but where they ought to go.

To teach is to learn twice.

A reader finds little in a book save what he puts there. But in a great book he finds space to put many things.

To know what we must do is good sense; to know what we must think is intelligence.

Imagination is that faculty which renders tangible what is intellectual, which incarnates what is spiritual — in a word, which makes visible, without distortion, that which of itself is invisible.

There are minds like convex and concave mirrors which reflect objects just as they receive them, but which never reflect them just as they are.

All great intellects have a certain lightness — as they possess wings to rise with, so do they have wings with which to go astray,

If one has dreaded too much an impending trouble, one feels some relief when the trouble finally comes.

To be interested in little things as well as in great, to be as ready for the one as for the other, is not weakness and littleness, but power and sufficiency.

That man is never mediocre who has much good sense and much good feeling.

There are hollow, sonorous minds, in which thoughts reverberate and echo as in a musical instrument. There are solid and flat minds, on which the most harmonious thought produces no effect other than the noisy blow of a hammer.

Tenderness is the repose of passion.

Few minds are spacious, few even have vacant places in them. Nearly all have capacities that are narrow and occupied by some knowledge which stops them up. To enjoy itself and let others enjoy it, a mind should always keep itself larger than its own thoughts.

Conceited people, like dwarfs, have the stature of a child with the face of a man.

Ambition is pitiless. Any merit that it cannot use is despicable in its eyes.

Children always tease and persecute what they love.

Think of the scores of people who drink, eat, and marry; buy, sell, and build; make contracts and guard their money; have friends and enemies, joys and sorrows; are born, grow, live and die — but are all the while asleep!

A man should select for his wife only such a woman as he would select for a friend, were she a man.

Children are well cared for only by their mothers; men, only by their wives.

The table is a kind of altar which ought to be decked on holidays and for festivals.

We should wear our velvet next the skin — that is, we should be the most amiable and agreeable to those of our own family.

Good manners and cheerful greetings are cards of invitation that circulate in all seasons.

No virtue ever appears small when acted on a large scale.

Wisdom is the science whereby we determine what is and what is not good for the soul. It is the science of sciences, for it alone can estimate true value, exact importance, proper use, what is dangerous and what useful.

Knowledge plus illusion is a combination that is the charm of life and art.

Education ought to be tender and severe, not cold and soft.

Necessity may make a doubtful action innocent, but it can never make it praiseworthy.

The greatest need of a people is to be governed; its greatest happiness, to be well governed.

Men have torn up the roads which led to Heaven, and which were trod by all the world. Now we must make our own ladders.

The one drawback with new books is that they prevent our reading old ones.

Ordinary fact or mere reality can never be the object of art. Illusion based upon truth is the secret of the fine arts.

Nothing is known well till long after it is learned.

The poet should not walk across an interval he can leap with a bound.

Words become luminous when the poet's finger touches them with its phosphorus.

Words are like glass — they obscure whatever they do not help us to see.

'Tis a great art to make of one's thought a balanced lance, hurl it, and impale it in the attention.

There are two monstrosities: passions of the mind, and ambitions of the body.

In the soul there is a taste for goodness, as in the body there is an appetite for pleasure.

He who fears pleasure is of finer stuff than he who hates it.

Minds that never rest are more than likely to go astray.

Minds are like fields: in some, the best is on the surface; in others, the best is at the bottom, often at great depth.

Though there are many moments hostile to truth, time and truth are friends.

The mechanism of speech may be compared to a bow, language being the cord which of itself projects the adjusted shaft. Speech is really a discharged arrow.

Superstition is the only religion of which base spirits are capable.

Politeness acts as a guard over the rough edges on our character, preventing them from harming others. We should never lay it aside, even in contact with coarse people.

Neither love nor friendship, respect nor admiration, gratitude nor devotion, should deprive us of our conscience and our discernment of good and evil. This is a possession we must never sell, which no price could ever purchase.

Truth gains character from the soul she inhabits. In arid souls she is rigorous and harsh, in loving souls she is tempered and gentle.

Write nothing, say nothing, think nothing which you do not believe is true before God.

Dare I say it? God may be easily known, if only it is not necessary to define Him.

Voltaire

WHOEVER said that self-love is the basis of all our emotions and actions was right; it isn't necessary to prove that men have faces, nor that they possess self-love. It is the instrument of our preservation: it is like a provision for perpetuating mankind; it is essential, it is dear to us, it is delightful, and it should be hidden.

Self-love is a balloon filled with wind, from which tempests emerge when pricked.

All joys do not cause laughter; great pleasures are serious: pleasures of love do not make us laugh.

Can you not seek the author of life but in the obscure labyrinth of theology?

It is strange that thought should depend upon the stomach, and still that men with the best stomachs are not always the best thinkers.

Jest with life: that is all it's good for.

A mountain being delivered of a mouse is quite as extraordinary, quite as worthy of admiration, as a mouse being delivered of a mountain. All the constellations in the universe could not bring forth a fly.

It is with books as with men, a very small number play a great part: the rest are confounded with the multitude.

A sovereign is called a tyrant who knows no law but his caprice.

With the world, do not resort to injuries, but only to irony and gaiety: injury revolts, while irony makes one reflect, and gaiety disarms.

Use, do not abuse: neither abstinence nor excess ever renders man happy.

Prejudice is the reason of fools.

It is difficult to free fools from the chains they revere.

Illusion is the first of all pleasures.

If as much care were taken to perpetuate a race of fine men as is done to prevent the mixture of ignoble blood in horses and dogs, the genealogy of every one would be written on his face and displayed in his manners.

I do not know in the whole history of the world a hero, a worthy man, a prophet, a true Christian, who has not been the victim of the jealous, of a scamp, or of a sinister spirit.

We never live: we are always in expectation of living.

A republic is not founded on virtue, but on the ambition of its citizens.

Virtue: a word easy to pronounce, difficult to understand.

It does not depend upon us to avoid poverty, but it does depend upon us to make that poverty respected.

History is the recital of facts represented as true. Fable, on the other hand, is the recital of facts represented as fiction. The history of man's ideas is nothing more than the chronicle of human error.

There must be some exquisite pleasure in governing, to judge from the numbers who are eager to be concerned in it.

The great man is more difficult to point out than the great artist. In an art or profession the man who has outdistanced his rivals is called great in his work, with reservations as to his character. But the great man must exhibit different merit. It is easier to say who are not great men than who are. They should have great virtues.

Divorce is probably coeval with marriage. Naturally, marriage is a few weeks more ancient; I believe men quarreled with their wives after five days, beat them after a month, and separated from them after six weeks.

There is but one morality, as there is but one geometry. You say that most men know little about geometry. True; but if they study it ever so little, they all draw the same conclusions.

Paradise was made for tender hearts; hell, for loveless hearts.

Superstition excites storms; philosophy appeases them.

If there were no God, it would be necessary to invent one.

Love is a canvas furnished by Nature, and embroidered by imagination.

Satire lies about men of letters during their life, and eulogy after their death.

Moderation is the pleasure of the wise.

Superstition is to religion what astrology is to astronomy: a very stupid daughter of a very wise mother.

All the reasoning of man is not worth one sentiment of woman.

It would appear that, in order to assure a just verdict in an action for adultery, the jury should be composed of six men and six women, and — in the event of a tie — a hermaphrodite to cast the deciding vote.

Young women who hang and drown themselves for love should be cautioned to reconsider, for changes in love are at least as frequent as in other affairs.

Age weakens the character; it is an old tree, producing only a few puny fruits — but always the same, acorns or apples.

Confucius did not invent a system of morals; he found it in the hearts of mankind.

Some there are who are so ashamed of all they do not know that they strive to disguise themselves either as wits or philosophers.

Speaking of government, does not its art lie in taking as much money as possible from one group of citizens to give it to another?

In religion zeal is a pure and enlightened attachment to worship of the Divinity and its maintenance and progress; but when it grows blind and false and takes to persecution, it becomes the greatest scourge of humanity.

The famous physician Dumoulin said when dying, "I leave two great physicians behind me, simple food and pure water."

When truth is disliked and reason is feared, a well-turned compliment succeeds better than inspired eloquence.

Shun idleness: it is the rust that attaches itself to the most brilliant metals.

46

There is no morality in superstition. There is none in ceremonial. It has nothing to do with dogma. Dogmas differ, but morality is the same among all men who make use of their reason. Morality proceeds from God, like light; superstition is only darkness.

In those countries where the morals are the most dissolute, the language is the most severe; as if they would replace on the lips what has deserted the heart.

The reasonable worship of a just God who punishes and rewards, would undoubtedly contribute to the happiness of men; but when that salutary knowledge of a just God is disfigured by absurd lies and dangerous superstitions, then the remedy turns to poison.

All thinkers have about the same principles, and form but one republic.

Finesse in wit consists of clouding a thought so that it may be all the more clearly perceived. It poses a sort of transparent enigma.

Poetry is the music of the soul.

Laws should never be in contradiction to usages; for, if the usages are good, the laws are valueless.

47

Pleasure has its time; so, too, has wisdom. Make love in thy youth, and in old age, attend to thy salvation.

All religions are more or less mixed with superstitions. Man is not responsible enough to content himself with a pure and sensible religion, worthy of the Deity.

Fine eyes are to the face what eloquence is to speech.

We can not always oblige, but we can always speak obligingly.

The best written book is a recipe for a pottage.

The wise Romans are particularly careful how they excommunicate the gentlemen who sing soprano in the opera, for it is bad enough to be castrated in this world without having to being damned in the other.

Love is of all the passions the strongest, for it attacks simultaneously the head, the heart, and the senses.

When you die, would you console yourself for parting from those with whom you liked to live? Think: they will be soon consoled for your death.

Three Ladies

GEORGES SAND

THERE are no more thorough prudes than those women who have some little secret to hide.

Life is as a slate where all our sins are written: from time to time we rub the sponge of repentance over it, in order to begin to sin anew.

Obstacles usually stimulate passion, but sometimes they kill it.

49

Whoever has loved knows all that life contains of sorrow and of joy.

The breaking of a heart leaves no traces.

The prayers of a lover are more imperious than the menaces of the whole world.

Women love always: when earth slips from them, they take refuge in heaven.

The world does not understand that we can prefer anything else to it.

Sorrow makes us very good or very bad.

To forgive a fault in another is more sublime than to be faultless one's self.

What is the world, or its opinion, to him who has studied in the lives of men the mysteries of their egotism and perfidy!

A woman can not guarantee her heart, even though her husband be the greatest and most perfect of men.

There is among men such intense affectation that they often boast of defects which they have not, more willingly than of qualities which they have.

The life of great geniuses is nothing but a sublime storm.

Oblivion is the flower that grows best on graves.

There are few souls who are so vigorously organized as to be able to maintain themselves in the calm of a strong resolve: all honest consciences are capable of the generosity of a day, but almost all succumb the next morning under the effort of the sacrifice.

It is the violence of their ideas and the blind haste of their passion that make men awkward when with women. A man who has blunted a little his sensations, at first studies to please rather than to be loved.

The greatest evidence of demoralization is the respect paid to wealth.

Solitude is the voice of Nature that speaks to us.

Heroes are men who set out to be demigods in their own eyes, and who end by being so at certain moments by dint of despising and combating all humanity.

Few are they who have been spared by calumny.

The misanthropist is to be pitied when his despair proceeds from an ardent love for the good, the beautiful, and the true.

The world takes away, from even the most candid heart, the freshness of faith and generosity.

Modesty is sometimes an exalted pride.

Vanity is the quicksand of reason.

MME. DE STAËL

Twenty years in the life of a man is sometimes a severe lesson.

Life often seems but a long shipwreck, of which the *débris* are friendship, glory, and love: the shores of our existence are strewn with them.

It is not enough to forgive: one must forget.

Many a man who has never been able to manage his own fortune, nor his wife, nor his children, has the stupidity to imagine himself capable of managing a nation.

The pleasures of thought are remedies for the wounds of the heart.

Sow good services; sweet remembrances will grow from them.

Glory can be for a woman but the brilliant mourning of happiness.

Men have made of Fortune an all-powerful goddess, in order that she be made responsible for all their blunders.

The egotism of a woman is always for two.

Time, which enfeebles criminal desires, leads us back to legitimate affection.

In hypocrisy there is as much folly as vice: it is as easy to be honest as to appear so.

Love, an episode in the life of man, is the entire story of the life of woman.

Frankness consists in always telling the truth, but not always all the truth.

Pretty women are like sovereigns: one flatters them only through self-interest.

However old a conjugal union, it still garners some sweetness. Winter has some cloudless days, and under the snow a few flowers still bloom.

MARGUERITE DE VALOIS

The less one sees and knows men, the higher one esteems them: for experience teaches their real value.

The more hidden the venom, the more dangerous it is.

We are always more disposed to laugh at nonsense than at genuine wit; because the nonsense is more agreeable to us, being more conformable to our own natures: fools love folly, and wise men wisdom.

There is no greater fool than he who thinks himself wise; no one wiser than he who suspects he is a fool.

There is in us more of the appearance of sense and of virtue than of the reality.

When one has a good day in the year, one is not wholly unfortunate.

Men are so accustomed to lie, that one can not take too many precautions before trusting them — if they are to be trusted at all.

The woman who does not choose to love should cut the matter short at once, by holding out no hopes to her suitor.

Love works miracles every day: such as weakening the strong, and strengthening the weak; making fools of the wise, and wise men of fools; favoring the passions, destroying reason, and, in a word, turning everything topsy-turvy.

He who knows his incapacity, knows something.

Extreme concupiscence may be found under an extreme austerity.

Hypocrites are wicked: they hide their defects with so much care, that their hearts are poisoned by them.

We shall all be perfectly virtuous when there is no longer any flesh on our bones.

I confess I should be glad if my pleasures were as pleasing to God as they are to me: in that case, I should often find matter for rejoicing.

A woman of honor should never suspect another of things she would not do herself.

Since love teaches how to trick the tricksters, how much reason have we to fear it — we who are poor simple creatures!

In love, as in war, a fortress that parleys is half taken.

It is because honesty will soon be scarce that we must use it to deceive the deceivers.

Pleasures are sins: we regret to offend God; but, then, pleasures please us.

The true and the false speak the same language.

It is difficult to repent of what gives us pleasure.

No one perfectly loves God who does not perfectly love some of his creatures.

Many weep for the sin, while they laugh over the pleasure.

There are women so hard to please that it seems as if nothing less than an angel will suit them: hence it comes that they often meet with devils.

God has put into the heart of man love and the boldness to sue, and into the heart of woman fear and the courage to refuse.

Love is a disease that kills nobody, but one whose time has come.

Stendhal

THE likelihood of constancy when desire is satisfied can only be foretold from
the constancy displayed, in spite of cruel
doubts and jealousy and ridicule, in the days
before intimate intercourse.

A man of sensibility, as soon as his heart is
touched, loses all traces of habit to guide his
action; and how can he follow a path, which
he has forgotten all about?

Passion-love carries us away in defiance of all our interests, gallant love manages always to respect them.

The vast majority of men, especially in France, desire and have a fashionable woman, in the same way in which a man gets a fine horse, as something which the luxury of a young man demands.

I have no doubt that a sensitive woman may come to the point of feeling no physical pleasure but with the man she loves. It is the opposite with the savage.

Such is the empire of modesty, that a woman of feeling betrays her sentiments for her lover sooner by deed than by word.

The glance is the great weapon of virtuous coquetry. With a glance, one may say everything, and yet one can always deny a glance; for it cannot be repeated textually.

Modesty is taught little girls very early by their mothers with such jealous care, that it almost looks like fellow-feeling; in this way women take measures in good time for the happiness of the lover to come.

The length of the siege humiliates a man; on the contrary it makes a woman's glory.

A woman of generous character will sacrifice her life a thousand times over for her lover, but will break with him for ever over a question of pride — for the opening or the shutting of a door.

The sight of all that is extremely beautiful in nature and in art recalls, with the swiftness of lightning, the memory of that which we love.

I have seen the most distinguished women charmed with a clever man, and, at the same time and almost with the same words, admire the biggest fools. I felt caught like a connoisseur, who sees the loveliest diamonds taken for paste, and paste preferred for being more massive.

The husband of a young woman adored by a lover — a husband whom she treats unkindly and scarcely allows to kiss her hand, has, at the very most, only the grossest physical pleasure, where the lover would find the charms and transports of the keenest happiness that exists on earth.

In France, most women make no account of a young man until they have turned him into a coxcomb. It is only then that he can flatter their vanity.

Women who are always taking offence might well ask themselves whether they are following a line of conduct, which they think really and truly is the road to happiness. Is there not a little lack of courage, mixed with a little mean revenge, at the bottom of a prude's heart?

Nothing is so interesting as passion: for there everything is unforeseen, and the principal is the victim. Nothing is so flat as gallantry, where everything is a matter of calculation, as in all the prosaic affairs of life.

Prudery is a kind of avarice — the worst of all.

The immense respect for money, which is the first and foremost vice of Englishmen and Italians, is less felt in France and reduced to perfectly rational limits in Germany.

For the soul of a great painter or a great poet, love is divine in that it increases a hundredfold the empire and the delight of his art, and the beauties of art are his soul's daily bread.

Real love renders the thought of death frequent, agreeable, unterrifying, a mere subject of comparison, the price we are willing to pay for many a thing.

The existence of great souls is not suspected. They hide away; all that is seen is a little originality. There are more great souls than one would think.

There is a delicious pleasure in clasping in your arms a woman who has wronged you grievously, who has been your bitter enemy for many a day, and is ready to be so again.

At the end of a visit you always finish by treating a lover better than you meant to.

A woman belongs by right to the man who loves her and is dearer to her than life.

The more desperately he is in love, the more violent the pressure a man is forced to put on himself, in order to risk annoying the woman he loves by taking her hand.

Sappho saw in love only sensual intoxication or physical pleasure made sublime by crystallization. Anacreon looked for sensual and intellectual amusement. There was too little security in Antiquity for people to find leisure for passion-love.

A man who trembles is not bored. The pleasures of love are always in proportion to our fear.

THIS VOLUME IS DESIGNED, PRINTED
AND PUBLISHED AT THE OFFICE OF
THE PETER PAUPER PRESS
MOUNT VERNON
NEW YORK